How We Use

Glass

Chris Oxlade

Raintree

Chicago, Illinois

Printed and bound in China by the South China
   Printing Company

08 07 06 05 04
10 9 8 7 6 5 4 3 2 1

Library of Congress Cataloging-in-Publication Data:
Oxlade, Chris.
  How we use glass / Chris Oxlade.
    p. cm. -- (Using materials)
Includes bibliographical references and index.
Contents: Glass and its properties -- Where is glass
from? -- Glass windows -- Glass in buildings -- Glass
colors and patterns -- Glass and heat -- Glass containers
-- Tough glass -- Glass mirrors -- Glass lenses-- Glass
fibers -- Optical fibers -- Glass in the environment.
  ISBN 1-4109-0594-2 (hc) 1-4109-0993-X (pb)
  1. Glass--Juvenile literature. [1. Glass.] I. Title. II.
Series:
Oxlade, Chris. Using materials
  TP857.3.O83 2004
  666'.1--dc21

                          2003007356

Acknowledgments
The publishers would like to thank the following for
permission to reproduce photographs:
p. 4 Nogues Alain/SYGMA/Corbis; pp. 5, 9 Rodney
Hyett/Elizabeth Whiting & Assoc./Corbis; p. 6 Larry
Stepanowicz/Visuals Unlimited; p. 7 ACE; p. 8 Andy
Arthur Photography; p. 10 Mark E. Gibson/Visuals
Unlimited; p. 1 Bob Rowan/Progressive Image/Corbis;
pp. 12, 13 Bob Zaunders/Corbis; p. 14 Maiman
Rick/SYGMA/Corbis; p. 15 Bob Krist/Corbis; pp. 16, 17,
18 William James Warren; p. 19 Drew Super
Photography; p. 21 Warren Stone/Visuals Unlimited;
p. 22 C/B Productions/Corbis; p. 23 Jonah Calinawan;
p. 24 James L.Amos/Corbis; p. 25 Liz King Media; p. 26
Inga Spence/Visuals Unlimited; p. 27 Alan
Goldsmith/Corbis; p. 28 Lewis Alan/SYGMA/Corbis;
p. 29 Stone/Getty Images.

Cover photographs reproduced with permission of
Corbis (top) and Corbis (Bob Witkowski) (bottom).

Every effort has been made to contact copyright
holders of any material reproduced in this book. Any
omissions will be rectified in subsequent printings if
notice is given to the publishers.

Contents

Glass and Its Properties 4

Where Does Glass Come From? 6

Glass Windows 8

Glass in Buildings 10

Glass Colors and Patterns 12

Glass and Heat 14

Glass Containers 16

Tough Glass 18

Glass Mirrors 20

Glass Lenses 22

Glass Fibers 24

Optical Fibers 26

Glass and the Environment 28

Find Out for Yourself 30

Glossary 31

Index 32

Any words appearing in bold, **like this,** are explained in the Glossary.

Glass and Its Properties

All the things we use at home, school, and work are made from materials. Glass is a material. It can be used for all sorts of different jobs. For example, we make ornaments from glass, we cover buildings with glass, and a type of glass even carries our e-mails around the world.

Glass lets light into these buildings but keeps out wind and rain.

Many people prefer colored glass for vases and bowls.

Properties tell us what a material is like. Glass can be **transparent,** which means light goes through it. This is a property of glass. Glass can also be clear or colored. It has a very smooth surface. It is hard but it is also **brittle,** which means it breaks before it bends. Air and water cannot flow through glass and neither can **electricity.**

Don't use it!

The different properties of materials make them useful for different jobs. For example, glass is brittle. So we could not use glass to make something that needs to bend, such as a bedspring.

Where Does Glass Come From?

Glass is not a **natural** material. It is made in factories. But the **raw materials** for glass are natural. They come from the ground. The main raw material is sand, the same as the sand on a beach. There are different kinds of glass. To make each different kind, different **chemicals** are added to the sand. Most glass is soda glass. It is made from sand, limestone, and a chemical called soda ash.

Glass is mostly made of sand. Sand is made up of tiny grains of **silica.**

When the liquid glass cools it turns to **solid,** clear glass.

Making glass

At a glass factory the ingredients are mixed together and poured into a huge tank. The glass **mixture** is heated to about 2,732 °F (1,500 °C), which is many times hotter than the temperature in a kitchen oven. The sand **melts** and mixes with the other ingredients. This makes hot, **liquid** glass.

The history of glass
People discovered how to make small glass things, such as beads, about 4,500 years ago. About 2,000 years ago glass blowing was invented. This is a way of making hollow glass things such as drinking glasses and vases.

Glass Windows

Most of the glass made in factories is used in windows. Glass is a good material for making windows because it is **transparent, waterproof,** and **airtight.** So a glass window lets light in, but it keeps out wind and rain. It also keeps warm air in, stopping a room from getting cold. Glass used in windows is called glazing.

There are two sheets of glass in a double-glazed window. The gap between them helps to stop heat from entering or leaving the building.

Opaque glass is made by blasting the glass surface with sand or by adding patterns.

Rough glass

We do not use plain glass in rooms that we do not want people to see into, such as bathrooms. Instead we use glass with a rough surface, called opaque glass. Opaque glass lets light in, but you cannot see clearly through it.

Making window glass

Windows are made from a type of glass called float glass.

To make float glass, melted glass is poured into a huge bath of a molten metal called tin. The glass spreads out on top of the tin to make a flat, thin sheet. The sheet is cooled very slowly, which keeps it from cracking.

Glass in Buildings

Some buildings are completely covered with glass. The glass hangs on the outside of the building in huge sheets. It makes the building look like a giant mirror. Some modern houses have glass walls instead of brick walls. This lets plenty of sunlight in, but means that people can see in from outside.

A layer of glass on the outside of a building is called a curtain wall because it hangs like a curtain.

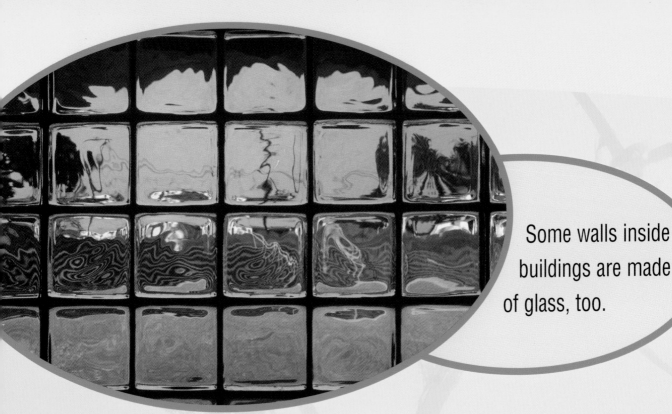

Some walls inside buildings are made of glass, too.

Keeping warm

Skyscrapers and office buildings are often covered with special kinds of glass that look silvery or gray. The sun gives us heat and light, but harmful rays also come from the sun. These special kinds of glass let heat and light into the building, but keep out the harmful rays. The glass also stops heat from escaping.

Don't use it!

*Glass can cover a building but it cannot hold a building up. Glass is hard but it is also **brittle.** It would break if we used it to build the frame of a building. Other materials, such as concrete and steel, are much better for this job.*

Glass Colors and Patterns

Many beautiful glass ornaments are made from colored glass. To make colored glass, special **chemicals** are added when the glass is made. Different chemicals create different colors in the glass. Light that shines through colored glass turns that color, too. If you look through colored glass, you can see to the other side, but everything there looks the same color as the glass.

A stained-glass window is made up of hundreds of pieces of colored glass.

An engraving wheel cuts slowly into the glass, making a groove.

Glass engraving

We can draw pictures and patterns on glass by engraving, or cutting, into it. Deep lines and curves are cut with a spinning disc. The surface can also be engraved with **acid** that eats away at the glass. This makes the surface look frosty. Engraved glass objects are often made from a sort of glass called lead glass, which is very sparkly.

Glass and Heat

When glass is heated to about 1,112 °F (600 °C) it begins to get soft. The more it is heated, the softer it becomes. When the temperature gets even hotter, the glass becomes a runny **liquid.** When it cools down it turns back to a **solid** again. Glass can be heated and cooled like this many times.

Bottles are made by pouring melted glass into a mold.

Glass containers are sometimes made by blowing down a pipe into a lump of melted glass. This is called glass blowing.

Shaping glass

Craftspeople who work with glass heat a piece of glass until it gets soft like caramel. Then they use different tools to stretch, flatten, or twist the glass into a shape. Glass objects such as bottles and drinking glasses are made in **molds.** Melted glass is poured into the mold and allowed to cool. When the mold is opened the new glass object is inside.

Glass for lights

Millions of light bulbs are made from glass every day. The bulbs are made by machines that puff air into small lumps of melted glass, blowing them up like bubble gum.

Glass Containers

Water and air cannot flow through glass. It is **waterproof** and **airtight.** These **properties** mean it is a good material for making containers such as drinking glasses, jars, and bottles. You must be careful with glass containers because they shatter easily if they are dropped.

Glass containers, such as drinking glasses, are made in **molds** so that they are all the same shape.

A test tube made from borax glass does not crack when it is heated up, even if it glows red-hot.

Chemical containers

Many **chemicals** that scientists use eat away materials such as plastic and metal. These chemicals cannot be stored in plastic or metal containers because the containers would leak. Most chemicals do not affect glass, so they can be safely stored in glass containers.

Glass in hot places

*Ordinary glass containers cannot be used for cooking. If they are heated up or cooled down quickly the glass cracks. Cooking containers are made from a special glass called borax glass that does not crack. **Test tubes** used by scientists are also made of borax glass.*

Tough Glass

Some types of glass are much stronger than the ordinary glass in windows and bottles. We use tough glass in places where the glass might be hit by something accidentally, such as glass doors and car windshields. Ordinary glass can shatter into sharp pieces. Tough glass does not shatter like this. If it does break, it breaks into small lumps.

This car windshield was made from laminated glass. It has cracked but has not fallen into pieces.

This glass has wire in the middle. The wire makes the glass very strong.

Tempering is a way of making ordinary glass into tough glass. To temper glass, the glass is heated up and cooled down slowly. Glass made by tempering is called toughened glass or safety glass.

Another way of making glass tough is to laminate it. A sheet of laminated glass is made of two sheets of glass with a layer of plastic in between them.

Glass Mirrors

A mirror is made from a flat sheet of glass with silver paint on the back. When you look in a mirror, light from your face goes through the glass. The light **reflects** off the silver paint, just like a ball bounces off the wall. Then the light comes back through the glass. Because the glass is so flat you see a perfect reflection of your face.

Mirrors show us what we look like.

Curved mirrors can make you look bigger or smaller, or a even strange shape.

See-through mirrors

Reflecting glass is a sort of flat glass that looks like a mirror. It has a layer of special **chemicals** on the surface. Most of the light that hits the glass bounces off, but a tiny bit goes through. A sheet of reflecting glass looks like a shiny mirror from one side but like normal glass from the other side. Reflecting glass is used in sunglasses and to keep bright sunlight out of buildings.

Glass Lenses

If you look through a glass object like a bottle or a glass, things on the other side look out of shape or blurred. This happens because light from the other side gets bent as it goes into the glass and out again. Scientists use this **property** of glass to make glass lenses. Lenses have curved faces so they bend light.

A magnifier has a glass lens. The glass bends light so that small things look bigger.

The glass lenses in eye glasses correct poor eyesight.

Devices such as microscopes, telescopes, binoculars, and cameras have lenses inside. The lenses are curved to make things look bigger or smaller, or to make photographs. Lenses are made from a sort of glass called optical glass. It is very clear so that all the light that hits it goes through.

Plastic lenses

*Glass lenses are expensive to make. Sometimes it is better to use cheaper plastic lenses instead. The plastic bends the light in the same way as glass does. For example, **disposable** cameras have plastic lenses instead of glass lenses. This means that the cameras are cheaper to make and buy.*

Glass Fibers

A **fiber** is a very thin piece of material. A glass fiber is a very thin piece of glass. Glass fibers are very strong if you try to pull them apart, but they snap easily if you bend them. We use glass fibers in different ways.

Glass fibers are made by pushing melted glass through tiny holes.

The hull of this boat is made of fiberglass. This is made by pouring plastic over glass fibers.

Glass fibers are made into fabric by **weaving.** Glass fiber fabric does not burn or melt until it gets extremely hot. It is used to make clothes for firefighters and blankets for putting out fires. Glass fibers are also bundled together to make thick, squashy matting. The matting is used for **insulation** in houses. It stops heat from escaping from the house.

Mixing with plastic

Glass fibers are mixed with plastic to make glass-reinforced plastic, or fiberglass. The glass makes the plastic extremely strong. Glass-reinforced plastic is used to make boats, car bodies, and water tanks.

Optical Fibers

An optical **fiber** is a special kind of glass fiber. It is made up of a glass fiber with a plastic coating on the outside. If you shine light into one end of an optical fiber the light bounces along the inside of the fiber and comes out the other end, like a tube. It works even if the optical fiber bends around a corner.

These optical fibers are part of a table lamp. Light from the bulb travels along the fibers and out of their tips.

There are many optical fibers inside an optical-fiber communication cable. The delicate fibers are protected from damage by a plastic coating.

Carrying messages

Optical fibers are very important for communications. Telephone calls, e-mails, and other sorts of information are changed to flashes of light that travel along optical fibers buried underground. A message can travel around the world through an optical fiber ten times in just one second! Thousands of telephone calls can travel together along a single optical fiber at the same time.

Glass and the Environment

The **raw materials** for glass are plentiful and easy to find. However, it takes a lot of energy to dig them out of the ground and to make them into glass. We can help to save this energy by using the glass again instead of throwing it away. This is called **recycling.** Recycling is important because glass does not **rot** when we throw it away in the trash.

Glass that is not thrown away properly is a danger to people and animals.

It is important to separate used glass by its color.

How glass is recycled

Most towns and cities have recycling bins where you can put used bottles and jars. The bins are taken to a recycling factory where the glass is crushed and melted to make new glass.

Don't use it!

*Most glass items can be made from recycled glass. However, recycled glass is not pure. We cannot use it in places where we need glass to be very pure such as for lenses and optical **fibers**.*

Find Out for Yourself

The best way to find out more about glass is to investigate it for yourself. Look around your home for places where glass is used, and keep an eye out for glass through your day. Think about why glass was used for each job. What **properties** make it suitable? You will find the answers to many of your questions in this book. You can also look in other books and on the Internet.

Books to read

Ballard, Carol. *Science Answers: Grouping Materials: From Gold to Wool.* Chicago: Heinemann Library, 2003.

Hunter, Rebecca. *Discovering Science: Matter.* Chicago: Raintree, 2001.

Using the Internet

Try searching the Internet to find out about things having to do with glass. Websites can change, so if one of the links below no longer works, don't worry. Use a search engine, such as www.yahooligans.com or www.internet4kids.com. For example, you could try searching using the keywords "glass blowing," "glass recycling," and "lenses."

Website

www.glassonweb.com/glassmanual
A fun site that explains how glass is made and used.

www.bbc.co.uk/schools/revisewise/science/materials/
A great site that explains all about different materials.

Glossary

acid liquid that can eat away at materials

airtight describes a material that does not let air pass through it

brittle describes a material that breaks very easily when it bends

chemical substance that we use to make other substances

disposable describes an object that is made to be thrown away after it is used

electricity form of energy that flows along wires

fiber long, thin, bendable piece of material

insulate to stop heat from escaping

liquid wet substance, like water, that you can pour

melt to turn from a solid into a liquid by heating it up

mixture substance made from two or more other substances mixed together

mold block of material with a space in the center. When molten glass is poured into the mold it cools and sets, making an object the same shape as the inside of the mold.

natural describes anything that is not made by people

property quality of a material that tells us what it is like. Hard, soft, bendable, and strong are all properties.

raw material natural material that is used to make other materials

recycle to use material from old objects to make new objects

reflect to bounce off. You see yourself in a mirror because light reflects from it.

rot to be broken down into simpler substances

silica substance found under the earth's surface and is one of the materials used to make glass

solid substance that is hard, something that is not a liquid or a gas

test tube glass tube with an open top and closed bottom

transparent describes a material that lets light pass through it

waterproof describes a material that does not let water pass through it

weaving making fabric by passing lengths of a material over and under each other